Extreme 3-D
Your Body

Human Eye

Alessandra Lacroix

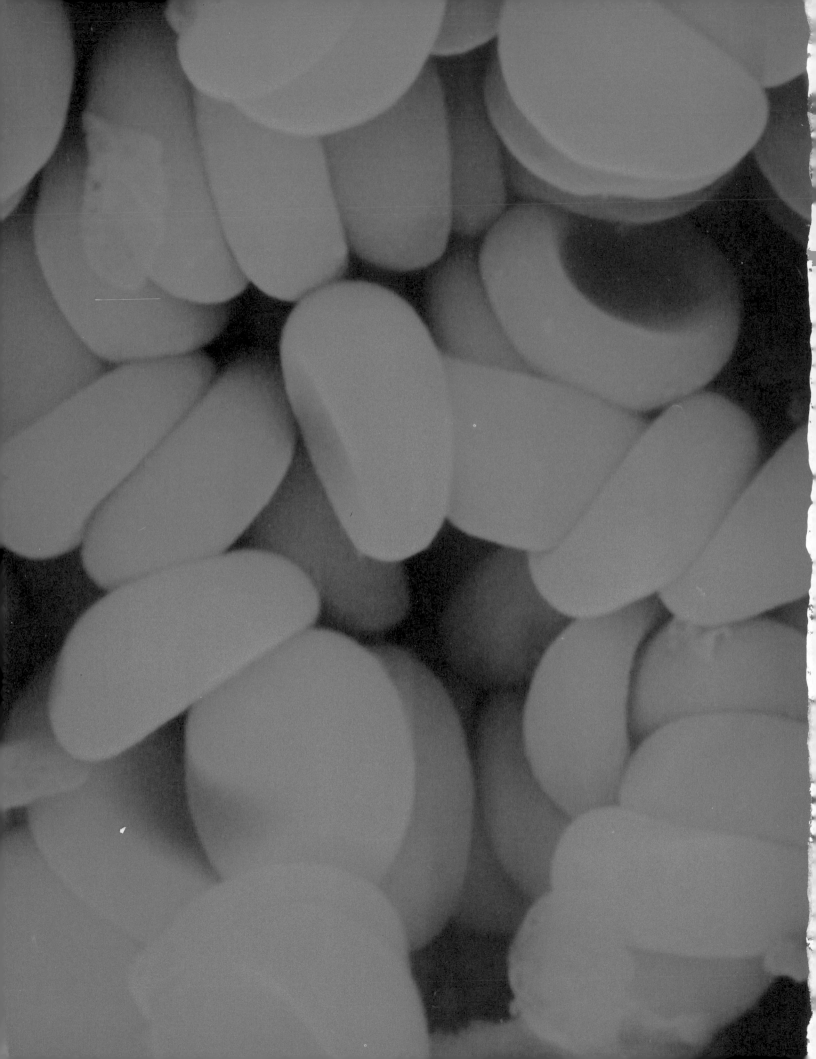

Extreme 3-D
Your Body

Written by
Shar Levine and **Leslie Johnstone**

SEM and Light Microscope Photography by
Dr. Elaine Humphrey

Tooth cavity

Dedication

S.L.—For my workout buddies Shira, Vicki, Sandra, Mary Ann, and Paula; and to the great body pump instructors, especially Trish and Cindy, who promise me that someday I'll have triceps that don't jiggle when I wave good-bye and who also assure me the torn rotator cuff will heal in time.

L.J.—For my sister, Holly, with much love.

E.H.—To Garnet and Derrick, my right and left hand, and the rest of the wonderful team who work with me in the BioImaging Facility.

Silver Dolphin

Silver Dolphin Books

An imprint of the Advantage Publishers Group
5880 Oberlin Drive, San Diego, CA 92121-4794
www.silverdolphinbooks.com

Text copyright © 2005 by becker&mayer!
Extreme 3-D: Your Body is produced by becker&mayer!,
Bellevue, Washington

www.beckermayer.com

If you have questions or comments about this product, send e-mail to infobm@beckermayer.com.

ISBN 1-59223-366-X

Produced, manufactured, and assembled in China.

1 2 3 4 5 09 08 07 06 05

04237

Edited by Don Roff
Written by Shar Levine and Leslie Johnstone
Designed by J. Max Steinmetz
SEM and light microscope photography by Dr. Elaine Humphrey
Illustrations by Roberto Campus, Ron Chironna, Dan Fell, Debbie Maizels, Erik Omtvedt, J. Max Steinmetz, and Christian Yah
Product development by Mark Byrnes
SEM colorization by Frank M. Young
Production management by Katie Stephens

Page 30: Tick © Department of Entomology, University of Nebraska-Lincoln

Acknowledgments

This book brings new meaning to the term "scavenger hunt." The authors spent countless hours hunting down various body parts and transporting these bits to the SEM lab at the University of British Columbia. No people were harmed in the writing of this book. Thanks to Linda Dempster and Ivan from the Eye Bank of British Columbia; Maureen Ashe; Dr. Alvin Nurnberg; Dr. Fred Mikelberg; Mr. Adam Isman; the staff at Just Ladies Fitness, especially Trish; Allen Larocque; May Lee; Charlotte Li; Sarah Ravn; Garnet Martens; Thoma Kareco; Megan Johnstone; Dr. Marietta Nelson; Cam Pye; Jennifer McQueen; and finally, John (Chip) Frostad.

Introduction

Even though you may have just hopped out of the bath, combed your hair, clipped your nails, brushed your teeth—and maybe even flossed them—the sad news is there's still lots of stuff left on your body. There are tiny microorganisms living on—and even in—your small frame. No matter how hard or how many times you try to wash or gargle, these things will still be with you.

"What kinds of things are on me and where exactly are they hiding?" you ask. This book will show you some of the bacteria, germs, and other creepy-crawly things inhabiting your body. Scientists estimate that you excrete billions of bacteria each day. While there seem to be a staggering number of bacteria living on you, if you could manage to scrape them all off, it would amount to a blob about the size of a pea. The bacteria volume you carry inside your body is much larger and would be about the size of a can of soda pop. Don't worry, it's not necessary to get back in the bath. Some of these bacteria are actually helpful.

Much of what you see on your body's surface is already dead. Flakes of dead skin fall off your body each day, eagerly devoured by tiny mites. The hair that you can see on your head is also dead. Your fingernails are dead, too. Let's take a closer look at your body. Along the way, you'll discover why it is important to wash your hands, brush your teeth, and protect your face from the sun.

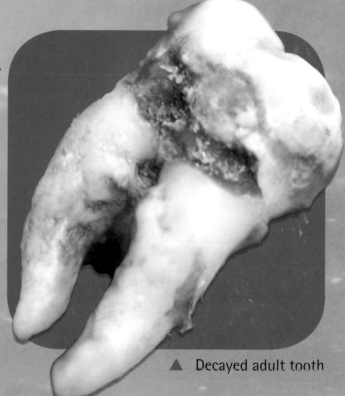

▲ Decayed adult tooth

CONTENTS

How We See in 3-D

We see in 3-D because we have two eyes. With both eyes placed at the front of our head, both eyes see the same object simultaneously and at slightly different angles. The position of our eyes also allows us to gauge distances easily.

For early humans, there were advantages to being able to judge distance. It makes it both easier to catch your dinner and avoid being made into lunch by wild beasts. Other animals— such as predatory birds that hunt for food—also have eyes at the front of their heads. Animals such as horses or cows, which graze and don't have to hunt for food, have eyes at the sides of their heads for a better view of potential predators. They simply need to see movement.

Some people can't see in 3-D. They may only be able to see with one eye, or they may not have the ability to combine the images seen with each of their eyes. These people must rely on other visual clues, such as position, size, or the way objects move, in order to judge distance. These are the same clues we use when we look at two-dimensional photographs, paintings, movies, or television.

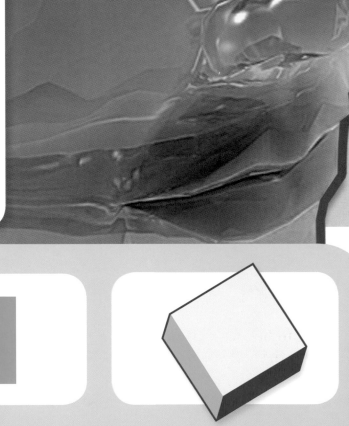

WHAT IS 3-D?

The "D" stands for "dimension," which is a measure in a single direction.

1-D: a line has one dimension, as it extends in a single direction.

2-D: a flat surface that has length and width, but no depth. In other words, two dimensions. An example of this is a painting or photograph.

3-D: an image that has length, width, and depth. Objects seen in 3-D look almost real.

The Red-Green Show

When you go to the movies, the images you see on the screen are flat. Some movies shown in special theaters (or with special projector lenses) feature 3-D effects, where things seem to fly off the screen and float in front of you. Some of these images are so real, viewers put their hands out and try to touch things that seem only inches away from their faces! To watch these 3-D movies, you have to wear special glasses. Some of these glasses have polarizing lenses that are dark gray, while other glasses have one red lens and one green (or blue) lens. These glasses allow the viewer to see the special effects.

Without the glasses, the image on the screen would be fuzzy—it would have a double image or appear to be outlined in red and green (or blue). Using the glasses allows each of your eyes to see a single, separate image. The pictures made using the red-green blurred outline are called *anaglyphic prints.*

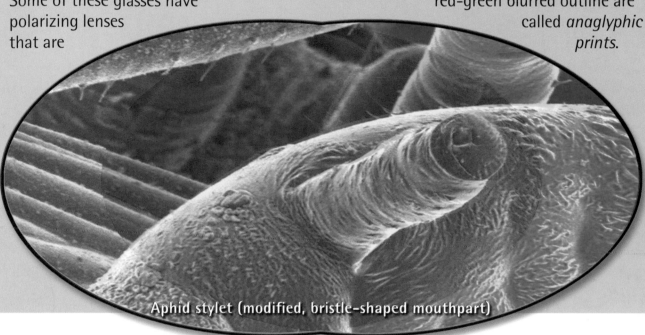

Aphid stylet (modified, bristle-shaped mouthpart)

The History of 3-D

It's hard to believe that the method you are going to use to view the exciting pictures in this book has been around for over 160 years! Sir Charles Wheatstone invented stereoscopic viewers in 1838. He got the name for his invention from the Greek words *stereos*, which means "solid," and *skopein*, which means "to view."

The invention of daguerreotypes, an early type of photograph, allowed Wheatstone to use stereo photographs in his viewer. These viewers and stereoscopic pictures were inexpensive and nearly every household owned one. They were used by both adults and children to view pictures from countries all over the world. As time went on, the pictures became geared toward kids—they depicted children's stories and fairy tales.

Stereoscopic viewer ▶

Microscopes

You may have used what is known as a compound light microscope. These microscopes are the type usually found in schools and homes. You look through an eyepiece to view a sample and see the light that shines from below the sample or onto the sample from the side. Compound light microscopes are very useful devices for seeing small objects. They are capable of magnifying objects several hundred times. A good-quality microscope of the type found in schools can usually magnify an object 400 times. A very high-quality light microscope can magnify an object at least 1,000 times.

The kind of microscope used to create the pictures in this book is called a *scanning electron microscope* (SEM). SEMs work by using a narrow beam of electrons. As this beam of electrons hits the sample, secondary electrons are given off from the surface of the sample. These are picked up by a secondary electron detector, which sends the image to a monitor. The narrow beam of electrons is scanned across the surface of the sample, hence the name. As the surface of the specimen is scanned, a computer is used to put the entire picture together on the monitor.

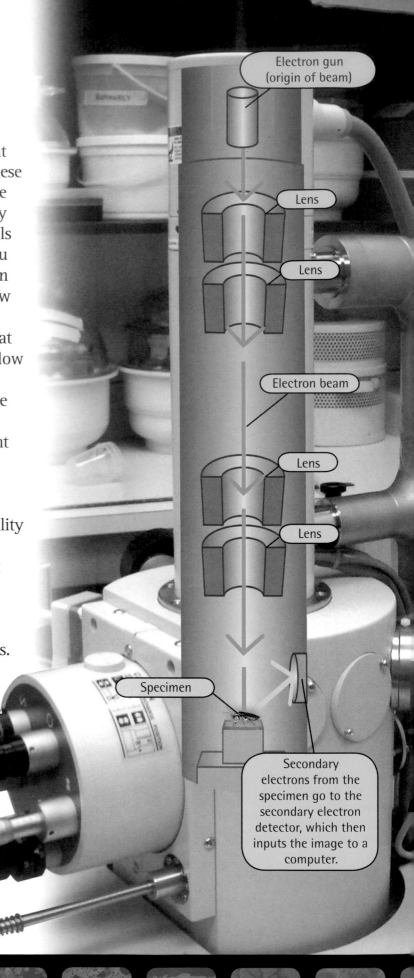

Electron gun (origin of beam)

Lens

Lens

Electron beam

Lens

Lens

Specimen

Secondary electrons from the specimen go to the secondary electron detector, which then inputs the image to a computer.

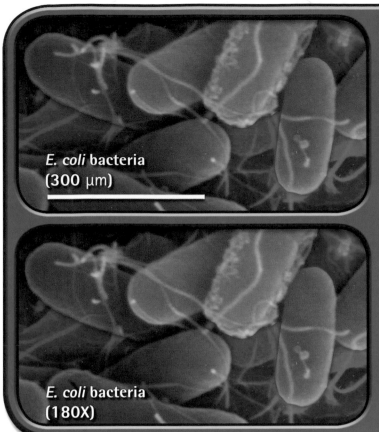

E. coli bacteria
(300 μm)

E. coli bacteria
(180X)

When you see an image like the one to the left in an advanced science book, there is usually a scale bar and a number followed by the letters "μm" to indicate the size of the specimen in micrometers, or thousandths of a millimeter. This scale bar is a kind of ruler used to measure the specimen in the picture. Scientists can calculate how large the specimen is using this information.

Due to the complex math involved in converting the size of the specimen (in micrometers) to the size of the image in the book, we have instead indicated the number of times the image was magnified.

So, rather than the measurement being given as "300 μm," for example, it has been given as "180X" to show that it has been magnified 180 times.

In the lab

In the laboratory, scanning electron microscopes allow scientists to see the surface of objects in incredible, dramatic detail. Fine structures on the surface of plants and animals, individual cells, miniscule bacteria and viruses, and even some larger molecules all become visible. These microscopes have a wide range of uses, from product testing to nanotechnology.

Other uses include:

→ Forensics: comparing the surfaces of objects or identifying samples of materials too small to see.

→ Product testing: looking at materials to see if there are miniscule cracks.

→ Art: believe it or not, there are some artists using SEM images as part of their artwork.

Feather shaft interior
(750X)

How to Make a 3-D Picture

STEP ONE: The specimen is placed under the lens of the scanning electron microscope.

To make 3-D pictures using a scanning electron microscope, we captured images of the samples on a computer. After the first picture was taken, we tilted the sample six to eight degrees and captured the second picture. We didn't have to worry about the sample moving on its own or about changes in the amount of light inside the chamber.

Also, since electrons don't have any color, pictures taken using electron microscopes are black and white. We used the computer to add different colors to the pictures.

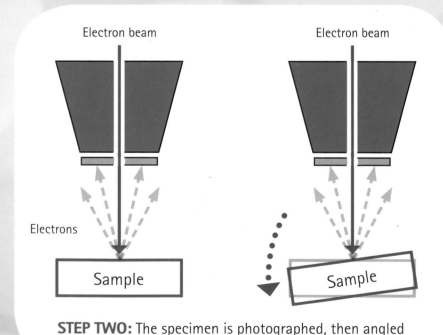

Electron beam

Electron beam

Electrons

Sample

Sample

STEP TWO: The specimen is photographed, then angled six to eight degrees and photographed again.

STEP THREE: With a computer, the two images of the specimen are colored: one in red and one in green.

We made the picture you would see with your left eye red; the picture your right eye would see is green. These two images are combined, one on top of the other. As a result, when you view them with the special glasses, the images appear in 3-D as long as you have the green lens over your right eye and the red lens over your left.

STEP FOUR: The red and green images are combined and the specimen is now seen as a 3-D image!

Skin

Your skin is your body's largest organ and is made up of layers: the *epidermis*, or outer layer, and the *dermis*, or inner layer. Your epidermis is the part of the skin you see—made up of flat, densely packed cells with no blood vessels. This layer of skin is protective: it keeps you in and invaders such as bacteria out. These cells can be different colors, giving you lighter or darker skin as well as freckles. The cells move from the inner part of the epidermis to the outside, where they are worn or scrubbed off. The inner layer of skin, the dermis, is where all the action is. This layer contains the blood supply for your skin as well as the hair follicles, muscles, fats, and glands.

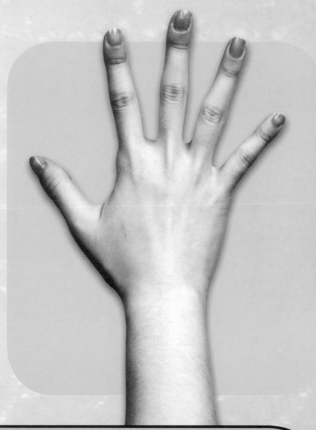

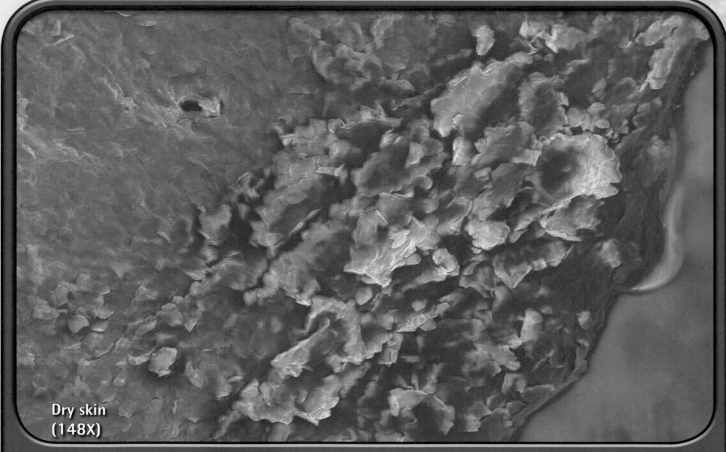

Dry skin (148X)

Dry skin is very common, particularly in the elderly. It occurs more frequently during the winter when cold air outside and heated air inside may decrease the humidity, or moisture in the air.

NEW AND OLD SKIN

Does all your skin look the same? If you could take an image of the skin on your hand and compare it to the skin on your rear end, you would be amazed at the difference. The skin covering your bottom—an area of your body that doesn't see the light of day—looks as smooth and soft as that of a baby. On the other hand (no pun intended!), the skin of your hand is much more rough. Why? The more your skin is out in the sun, the more it is damaged.

New skin
(188X)

Old skin
(188X)

Did you know?

Your body is held together by a kind of glue called *collagen*. If you want to see an example of collagen, you can look at the gristly part of red meat. While your bones give your body its shape, the collagen joins the bones together. Without this substance, we would fall apart, as there would be nothing to hold our bones together.

And yes, this is the same stuff you see advertised in magazines as a beauty treatment. Collagen can be injected into the skin to help get rid of wrinkles.

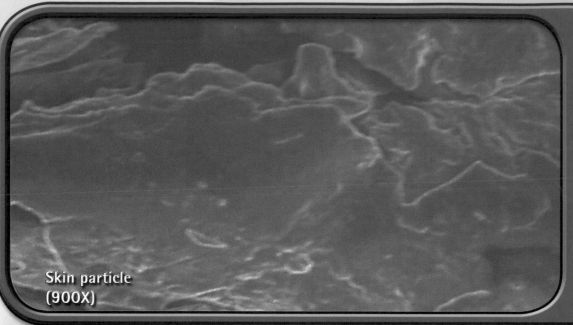

**Skin particle
(900X)**

Did you ever wonder why you don't have hair on your palms? Thick skin, like that found on your palms or the soles of your feet, doesn't have hair follicles and is not as soft or elastic as the skin on the rest of your body.

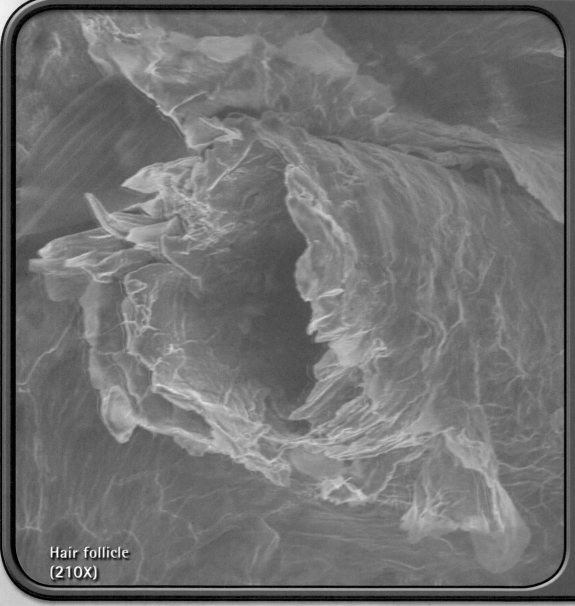

**Hair follicle
(210X)**

Let's talk about that flaky stuff on your head. The skin on your scalp is different from the skin on the rest of your body. You shed dead skin cells and hair. The only skin you notice when it falls off is probably the white stuff from your head: dandruff. If you really want to be technical, you could use the term *seborrheic dermatitis*.

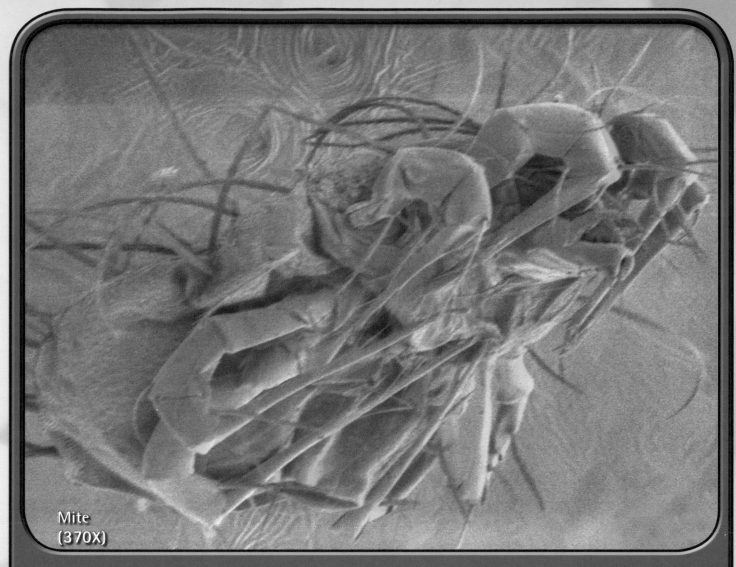

Mite
(370X)

Dust particles
(2,280X)

LESS FILLING, TASTES GREAT

The lowly mite loves dining on your dead skin. All the stuff that flakes off your body, including from your head, is a gourmet delight to a mite. These eight-legged little guys are related to spiders, but they don't spin webs. They are usually picked up by your vacuum cleaner, although they are known to hide in your bed linens. If you have dust allergies, it is probably due to these wee beasties. It's not only the dust mites that are bothering you, it's also their poop. Aren't you glad we told you that?

Sweat

If you say that something is "no sweat," it means that it's really easy. But what is sweat? Sweating, it turns out, is good for you. The smell may be unpleasant for those close to you, but that's not your problem. Let's take a close look at sweat.

Human body sweat

Clean clothing
(420X)

Dirty clothing
(420X)

THE SHIRT OFF YOUR BACK

You start out your day with a clean, fresh-smelling T-shirt and return home after playing all day to discover that your clothes are filthy.

Compare these two images. On the left is a close-up of a clean T-shirt. You can see that there's no dirt on the cotton fibers or in the weave of the fabric. However, the shirt on the right . . . what is all that stuff? Sweat!

More than just water dripping out from your pores, sweat consists of water, salt, and small amounts of other chemicals your body excretes.

Check out the cubes on the dirty shirt. That's salt and yes, it comes from your body. The rest of the stuff in the image is also from your body. You can see dirt, grease, and the other goo that sticks to the sweat on your body and rubs off on your shirt. Scientists think that there may also be small amounts of antibiotic proteins in sweat that help the body protect itself from harmful bacteria.

YUM!

Sweat may gross you out, but mosquitoes find it very attractive. These bloodsucking insects consider your sweat an invitation to a buffet. Two chemicals in human sweat, 3-methyl-2-hexenoic acid and 7-octenoic acid, act as a dinner bell for hungry mosquitoes.

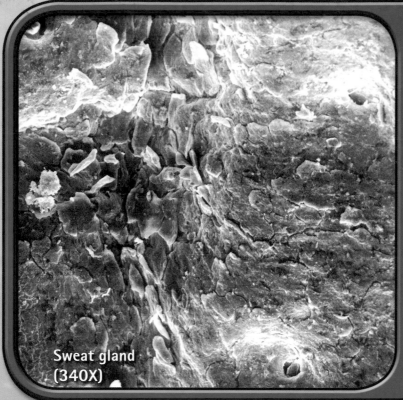

Sweat gland
(340X)

You have a significant number of sweat glands. How many? Anywhere from 2.5 to 4 million glands all over your body. Your feet, palms, head—just about every spot on your body—will sweat.

WHY DO WE SWEAT?

When you exercise or when you are hot, you need to cool down. Sweating is how your body controls its temperature. As you sweat, the water in your sweat evaporates, or changes into water vapor, which causes the temperature of your skin to come down slightly, cooling your body.

Scabs

Don't pick at that scab! Has anyone ever said that to you? If you couldn't form scabs on your skin, all your blood would ooze out through any little cut. Exactly how does your body form a scab?

Scab on a scraped elbow

When you have a cut or a scrape, tiny blood particles, or *platelets*, attach to the site of the wound. Fibers of collagen in your blood bond to the platelets and a plug forms. The platelets break apart and release chemicals that cause the tiny blood vessels to constrict, or become narrower, which stops the bleeding. The platelets also release proteins that combine with calcium and other chemicals in the blood to form *thrombin*. The thrombin breaks down large particles in the blood called *fibrinogen*, which forms a sticky protein called *fibrin*. The scab that forms is mostly fibrin fibers, bits of platelets, and red and white blood cells. The scab gets smaller and pulls in the edges of the wound, until eventually it falls off. Don't pick that scab—let your body do its job!

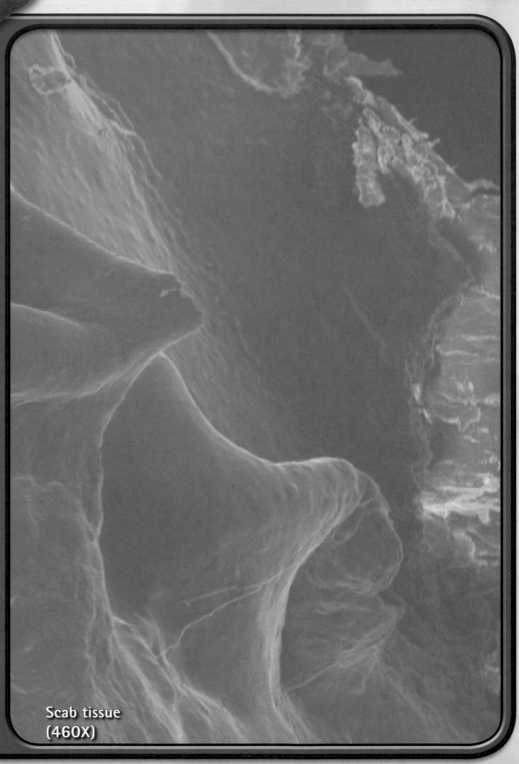

Scab tissue (460X)

There are several different chemicals in your blood, called *factors*, and if some of these factors are missing, you won't have normal clotting, which can be a health risk. You can also use up all your clotting factors if you have an injury that bleeds a lot, causing your blood to stop clotting.

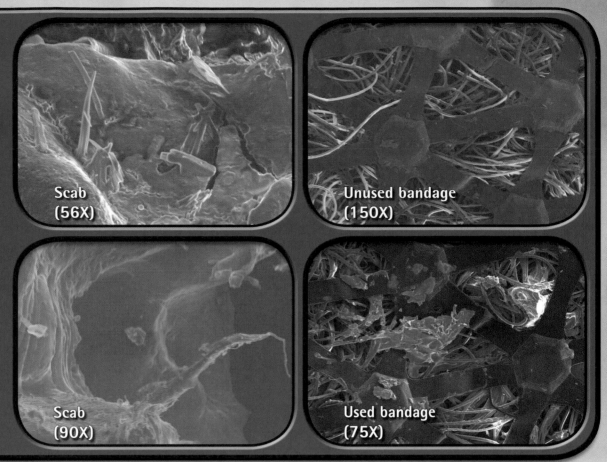

Scab (56X)

Unused bandage (150X)

Scab (90X)

Used bandage (75X)

Did you know?

When scientists want to look at only one part of the blood, they put the blood into a mechanical device called a *centrifuge*. The blood in a test tube is spun around very quickly and it forms layers inside the test tube. Whole blood will form three layers: one containing plasma, or the liquid part of the blood; one containing red blood cells; and one containing white blood cells and platelets, which is called the "buffy coat."

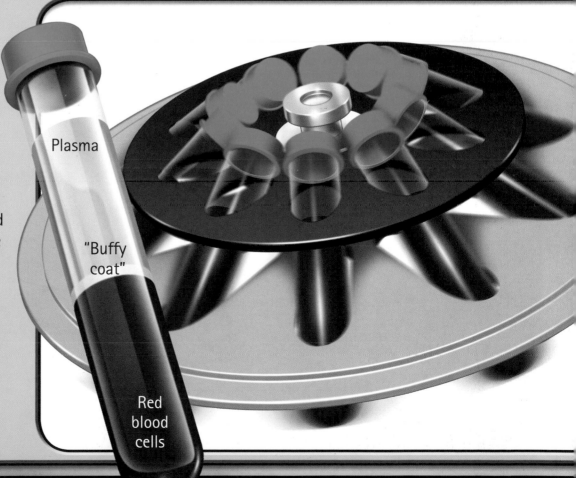

Plasma

"Buffy coat"

Red blood cells

Nails

Check out the nails on your fingers and toes. If you have a cat or dog, look at its paws. Does it have nails, too? Maybe your pet's feet don't look much like yours, but it does have nails. Aren't you glad you don't have nails like your dog's? Wearing sneakers would really be a pain! What exactly are nails, though?

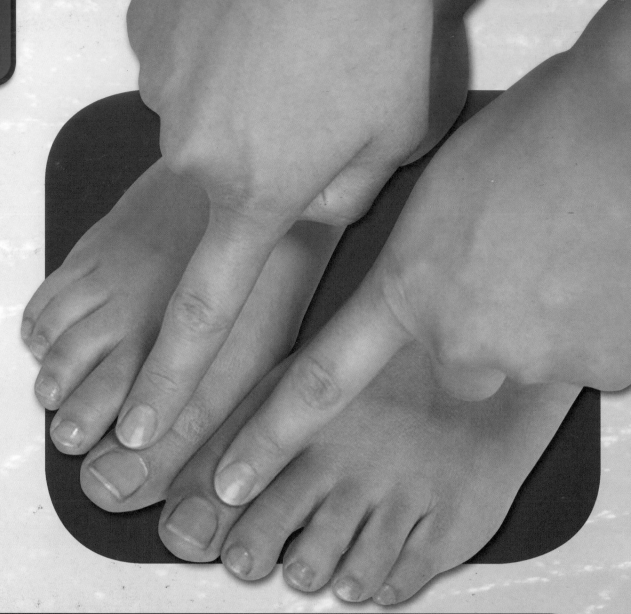

Human fingernail (68X)

ANATOMY OF A FINGERNAIL

Unless you have had an accident where you crushed a nail and it fell off, the ends of your fingers and toes should be covered with this protective layer.

If you examine your fingernails, the bottom part of your nail, the *body*, covers the nail bed. The tip of the nail is called the *free edge*. This is the area that you file and clip. The part of the nail that you can't see because it is inside your skin is the *root*. The tissue that you occasionally push back at the base of the nail is called the *cuticle*. The white, moon-shaped area at the bottom of your nail is called the *lunula*.

WHY YOU SHOULD WASH YOUR HANDS BEFORE EATING

Before eating, do you take time to wash your hands? Maybe this image will make you think twice before putting your unwashed fingers into your mouth. While you can't see them, there are germs and bacteria on the surface of just about everything you touch. Most of these are harmless, but some (see *E. coli*, page 42) can make you really sick.

You should wash your hands each time you use the bathroom. Health experts recommend that after you apply soap to your hands, you should rub them back and forth for as long as it takes you to sing "Happy Birthday" or the alphabet song slowly. Always wash with soap!

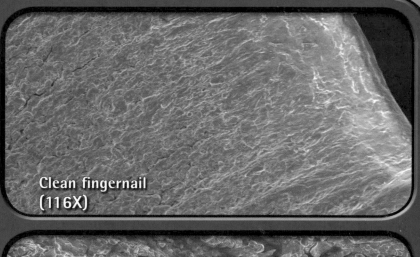

Clean fingernail (116X)

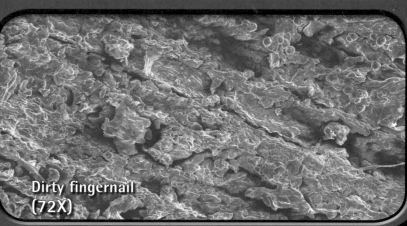

Dirty fingernail (72X)

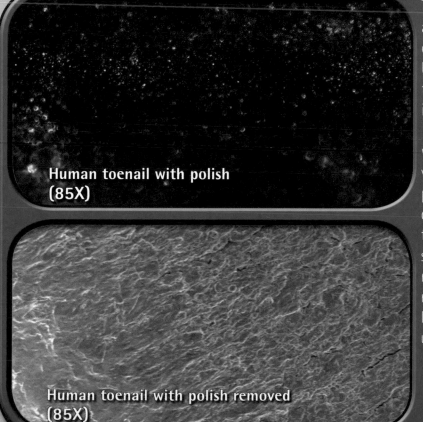

Human toenail with polish (85X)

Human toenail with polish removed (85X)

This is what nail polish looks like under a microscope. It contains tiny beads of different colors. When the light hits the beads it reflects the color of that bead, thus making it look like the nail polish is changing color.

The image at the bottom shows what happens to your lovely nails after you have taken off your nail polish. Nail polish contains chemicals that won't dissolve in water. Instead, to remove the polish you need to use a solvent, such as acetone, which can dry out your nails and make them brittle. Always use nail polish remover in a well-ventilated location and wash your hands after using it.

Hair

HAIR ON YOUR BODY

Before you jump into the bath, take a look at yourself without any clothes on. Your body is covered with hair. The hair on your arms is probably fine and short and may be difficult to see, while the hair on your head (assuming you haven't shaved it off) is thick and long. It may not be really long, but it's certainly longer than the hair on your toes. You may even have hair on your legs or under your arms. As you get older, you will get even hairier, sprouting hair inside your ears and on your face. If you're a guy, you may grow hair on your chest and down your back.

Is there hair everywhere? No. The palms of your hands, the soles of your feet, and your lips haven't got any hair.

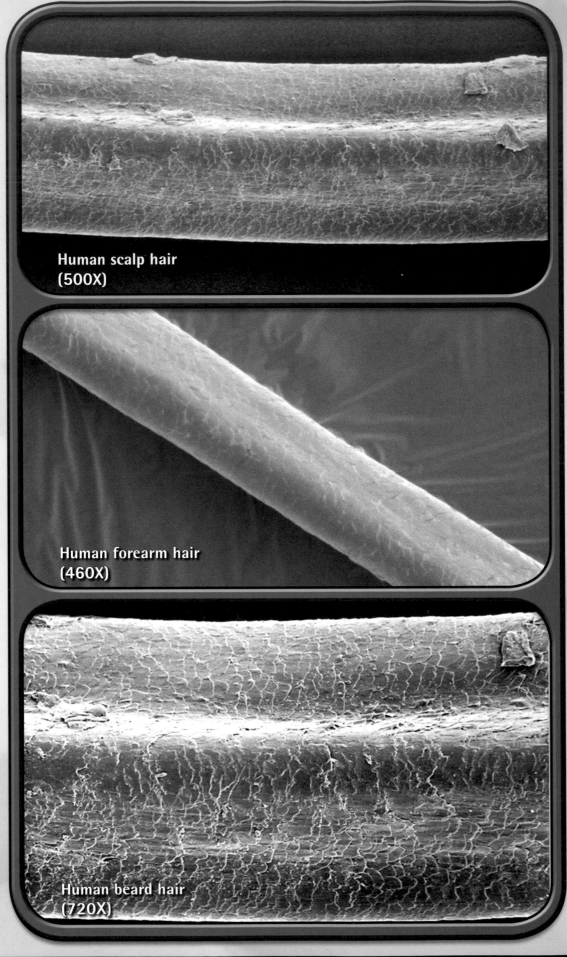

Human scalp hair (500X)

Human forearm hair (460X)

Human beard hair (720X)

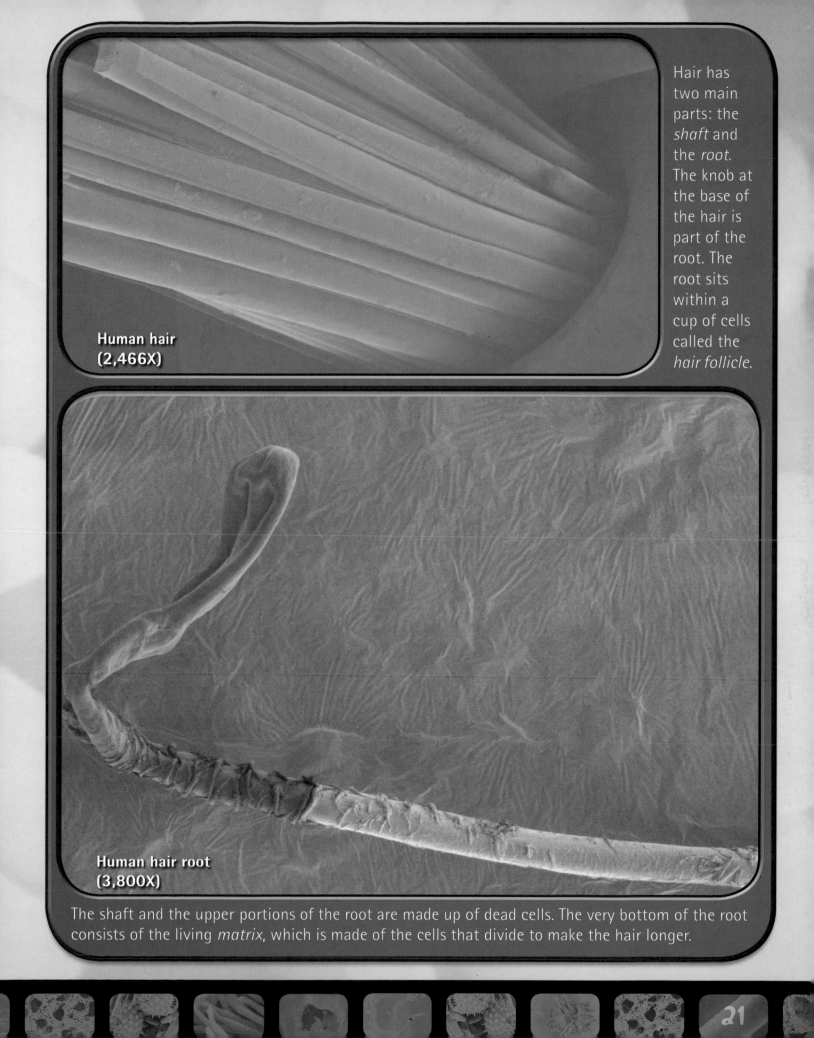

Human hair (2,466X)

Hair has two main parts: the *shaft* and the *root.* The knob at the base of the hair is part of the root. The root sits within a cup of cells called the *hair follicle.*

Human hair root (3,800X)

The shaft and the upper portions of the root are made up of dead cells. The very bottom of the root consists of the living *matrix*, which is made of the cells that divide to make the hair longer.

Cuticle
(1,320X)

When a shaft of hair is cut across, it is possible to see that the hairs are made up of two or three layers of cells. The outside coating is called the *cuticle*. The cuticle is a single layer of overlapping, transparent cells. Sometimes this layer can look scaly. In some types of hair, depending on color, there is an area in the center of the hair containing shrunken cells and large air pockets. This is called the *medulla*. The main inside layer of the hair is the *cortex*.

Straight hair
(1,270X)

Curly hair
(440X)

SPLIT ENDS

The cortex is made up of twisted proteins that allow the hair to stretch. If you abuse your hair, you can wear off some of the cuticle and expose the cortex. When this happens the cortex begins to unravel and the ends of your hair look frayed or "split." You can't grow a new covering, and the only way to get rid of the split ends is to cut them off. The cortex is also responsible for your hair's color and texture.

DIFFERENT KINDS OF HAIR

Is your hair naturally straight or curly? Does it fall into lovely waves or frizz after you have washed it? Use a magnifying glass to compare the hair shaft of a friend who has curly hair to that of a friend who has straight hair, and another who has blond or red hair. Do their hairs look the same? Some hair follicles are large and the hair is probably thick. If a person has small follicles, her hair is most likely fine or thin. The follicle determines the type of hair a person has.

Blond hair

Brown hair

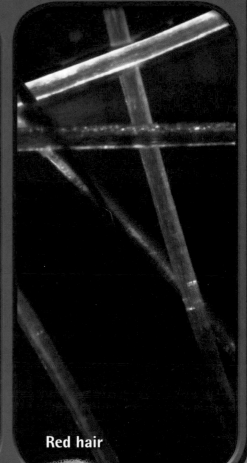
Red hair

GOING GRAY

Do you have brown hair? Red? Blond? Some other color that can't be easily described? Has your hair color changed from when you were in diapers to a darker shade of brown or blond? When your hair is being made in your follicles, a type of cell called a *melanocyte* makes the melanins, or colored chemicals, that give your hair its color. The melanin extends through the hair cortex and is what makes each strand of hair look blond, red, brown, or black. The darker your hair, the more melanin it contains. White hair has no melanin at all. As you become older, the melanocytes stop working and your hair turns white or gray.

Fleas

If you have a dog or cat, you know that at certain times of the year your animal brings home its own pets: a coat full of fleas. It may be comforting to know that your pet isn't the only animal that attracts fleas: any kind of mammal or bird can serve as dinner for these creatures.

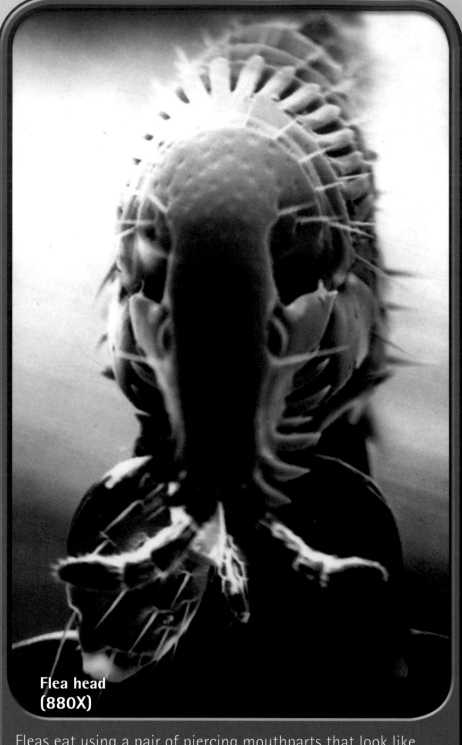

Flea head (880X)

Fleas eat using a pair of piercing mouthparts that look like big buck teeth. Fleas are the vampires of the insect kingdom: they use these huge "fangs" to suck up your blood. They can also leave behind bacteria. Fleas were responsible for killing millions of people in the Middle Ages. During this time, fleas that lived on rats spread the Black Death—or plague—which killed more than one quarter of the human population of Europe!

HOW HIGH CAN YOU GO?

Fleas are superior jumpers. If you could jump as far for your size as a flea can, you would be able to leap about 600 feet! Fleas have a pad of rubbery material called *resilin* that they compress. When the pad is released (like releasing a stretched rubber band), they use it to fling themselves great distances through the air to land on a new host—namely you!

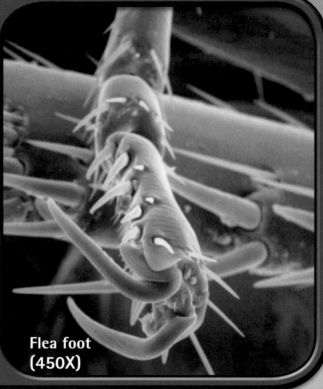

Flea foot (450X)

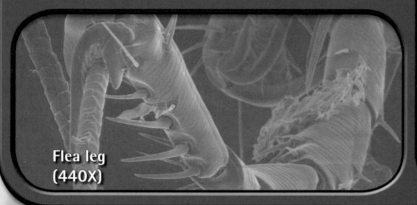

Flea leg (440X)

HOOKED UP

These little creatures have tough bodies for protection against their hosts. Not only do the hooks keep the fleas in place, but their hard shells guard them against teeth, claws, and brushes. They can live for long periods of time without eating and can survive in very hot and cold temperatures.

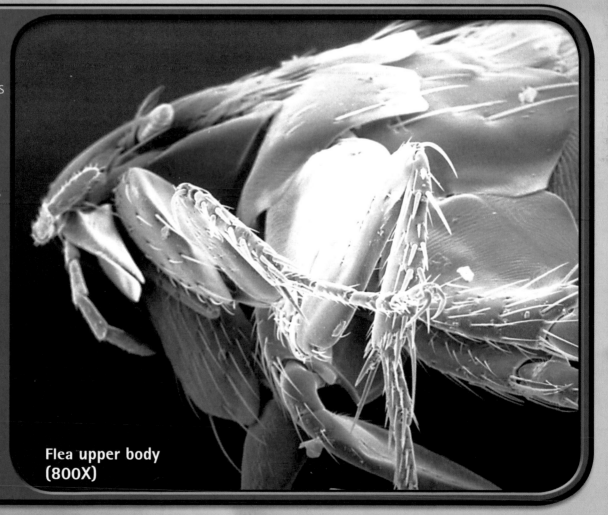

Flea upper body (800X)

Eyes

These are parts of your body you can't see, but you need them to see. These are your eye's rods and cones—without them, the world would be a darker and less colorful place.

Your eye has different layers. At the front is the cornea. Behind the cornea is an interior chamber filled with a liquid called the *aqueous humor*. Going deeper is the iris, or colored part of the eye. The iris opens and closes like the shutter of a camera. Every shutter needs a lens and your eye has one, too. Behind the lens is the vitreous chamber, where you will find the jellylike *vitreous humor*.

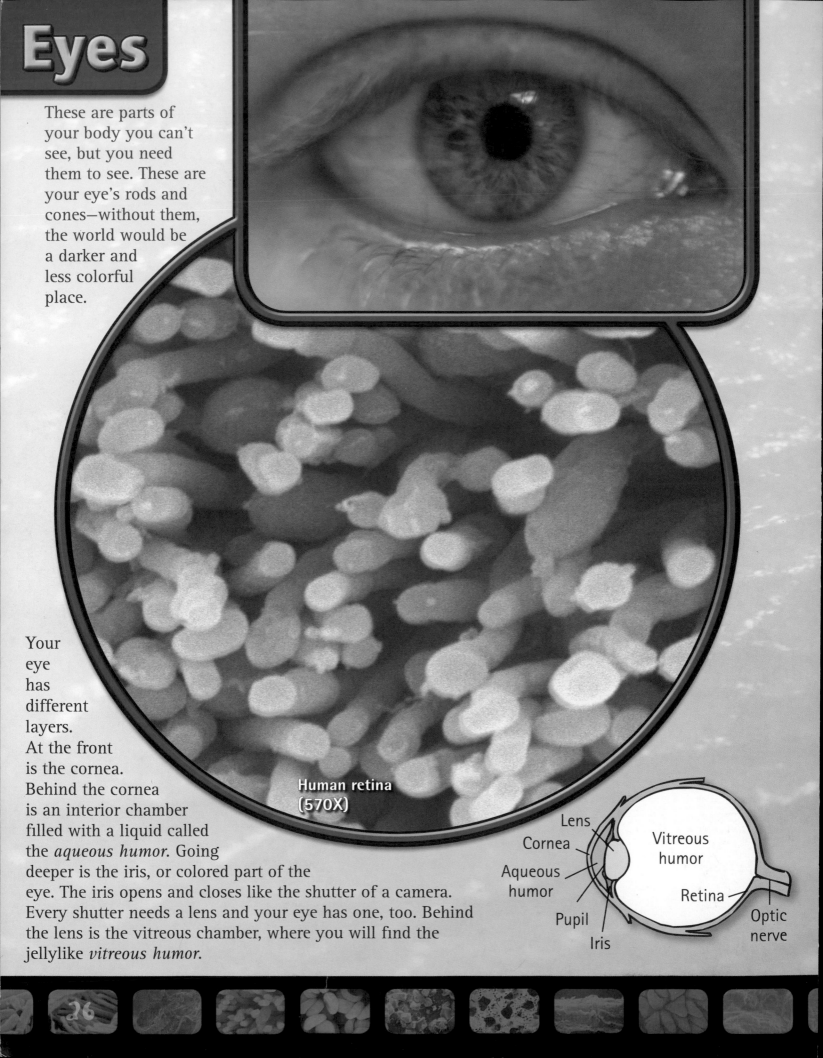

Human retina (570X)

Lens
Cornea
Aqueous humor
Pupil
Iris
Vitreous humor
Retina
Optic nerve

Human rods and cones (570X)

So what do the rods and cones do? These are the sensory cells of the eye. They change chemically when light hits them; this chemical change causes a nerve impulse to form and travel to the brain. Take a look at the image above—can you find the cones? The cones look like ice-cream cones (upside down) and they help you see fine details and colors. The rods stand straight up and look like cylinders. The rods help you see when it is dark. What makes rods different from cones, other than their shape, is that rods are much more sensitive to light but not to color, and are therefore used more in dim light. Cones change with different hues of light, allowing us to see colors. If you had only rods, you would see everything in black and white, but you would have very good night vision.

Human eye lens

Human eye lens: Human lenses naturally cut out ultraviolet light so it doesn't burn the retina. When doctors first started implanting artificial lenses, some ultraviolet light went through the lens and patients could see extra color. Of course, this wasn't a good thing for their retinas. Later, improved artificial lenses were better at reducing the harmful ultraviolet light.

Fish eye lens

Fish eye lens: Fish have spherical lenses, forming a circle if cut across. Our lenses have a flattened, spherical shape, so if they were cut across they would appear slightly oval in shape. In other words, fish lenses look like gumballs and ours look more like throat lozenges.

Eyelashes

Some people have long, thick lashes, while others just wish they had long, thick lashes. Other than helping you look cute, your eyelashes serve a useful purpose. Without eyelashes to protect you, dust and dirt would blow into your eyes and sweat would drip into your orbs, too.

Clean eyelash (40X)

Dirty eyelash (20X)

EYES OF THE PAST

How long have people been using mascara? If the ancient Egyptians were any indication, using a product to make your eyes look bigger goes back a long way. Check out the makeup on the King Tut sarcophagus. There's more eyeliner than most rock stars wear on stage! The Egyptians wore eye makeup made from galena (a bluish-gray mineral) and other ingredients.

King Tut sarcophagus

Skip forward to 1913, when Mabel Williams received a cool gift from her brother, T. L. He whipped together some coal dust and petroleum jelly, and voilà—the first mascara was born. This product launched the Maybelline cosmetics empire.

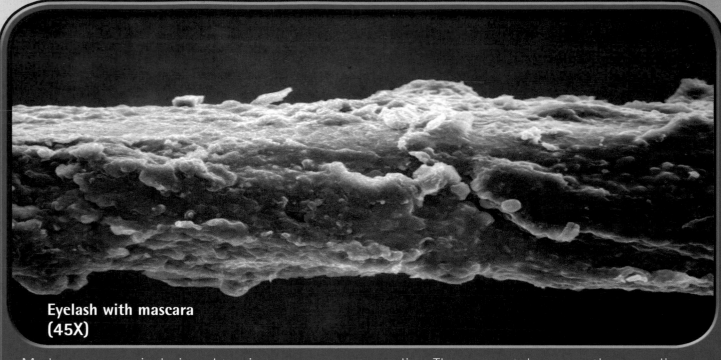

**Eyelash with mascara
(45X)**

Modern mascara is designed to give you long, thick lashes that don't stick together. Preservatives are added to keep the mascara from growing bacteria and to prevent bugs from growing inside the mascara tube.

Much like the hair on your head, eyelashes can get bugs—very tiny bugs. These tiny bugs are lice. They are not, however, the same lice that clamp onto your hair. You cannot get rid of these lice the same way you treat your hair. If you did, chemicals from the shampoo could harm your eyes. Instead, these lice need to be smothered with something thick and gooey, like petroleum jelly.

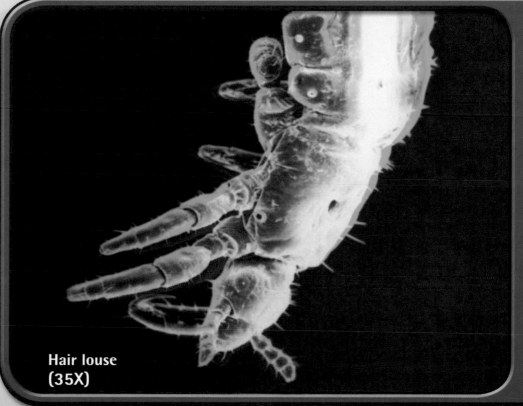

**Hair louse
(35X)**

These lice live on your lashes. If you have really good eyesight, you might even be able to spot them with the naked eye—but you might not want to get too close. They anchor themselves to your lashes and lay eggs on the tiny hairs. If allowed to breed undisturbed, they can cause your lashes to fall out. Not to worry, though—you will grow a new lash. In case you were wondering, these creatures are called *demodicids*.

Ticks and Lice

Imagine a creature that buries its head in your skin, then begins to dine on your blood. Meet the tick, a vampire relative of the spider and scorpion. And while a veterinarian may treat your pet for fleas and ticks, these two pests are not in the same family.

Ticks can range in size from a sesame seed to the end of a pencil eraser. Unlike other arachnids, ticks' bodies are in one piece. The pincerlike legs help keep the tick firmly attached to its victim.

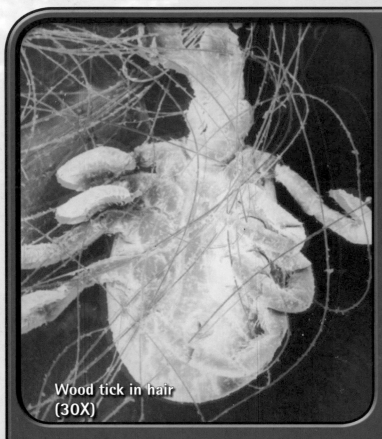

Wood tick in hair (30X)

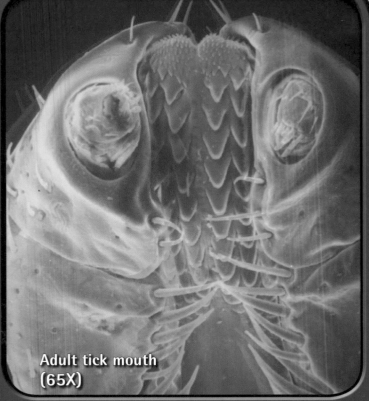

Adult tick mouth (65X)

Ticks don't fly onto their hosts. They hang around on just about any kind of surface and wait until their food walks by. When it senses vibration, shadow, or movement, or detects the exhaled breath of a creature, the tick simply grabs onto the skin or hair of a passing victim.

Ticks have rasping mouthparts that dig or burrow into skin and anchor the beast to their living buffet. To remove a tick from your skin, put pressure on its head by squeezing it like a pimple. Don't pull on the abdomen (the part sticking out), as it will break off, leaving the head under the skin. Keep the tick's body on a damp cotton ball, in a closed, sealable plastic bag, in case doctors need to identify it.

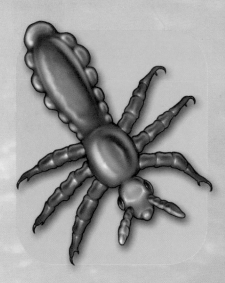

DISEASE CARRIERS

Lice are parasites: like ticks and fleas, they live off the blood of their hosts. They also carry diseases such as typhus, which is a deadly disease that affects people in warm, overcrowded, and underdeveloped countries such as China. Typhus can cause symptoms such as high fever, delirium, headaches, and rashes. People can get shots to inoculate themselves against this disease.

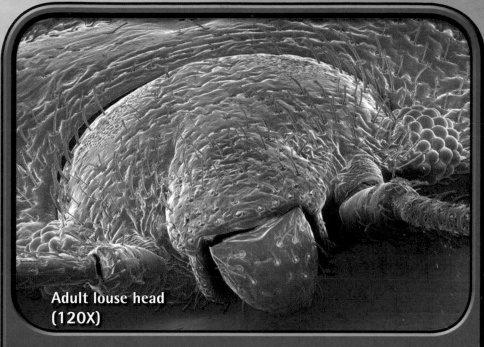

Adult louse head (120X)

TINY BLOODSUCKERS

Lice are tiny, eight-legged creatures, like spiders. Most are only a few millimeters in length, but the largest species of lice can be almost one centimeter long. They have teeth that can cut through your skin so that they can pump out blood from small blood vessels. Lice eggs are cemented onto the host's hair or feathers. Lice can also live in your clothes. They can be transmitted by stray hairs or by borrowed hats and hairbrushes. Also, if you ever come home from the outdoors with lice, it is not because you haven't washed your hair; it's because lice are highly contagious. Bites cause red bumps to form, and if you scratch them the skin can become broken and infected. Don't scratch—get medical treatment at once!

Did you know?

Birds can't go to the store and buy special soaps and shampoos to get rid of their lice. Instead, some types of birds pick up ants and place them between their feathers. The ants give off a fluid that kills the lice and causes them to fall off the birds. This process is called "anting."

Teeth

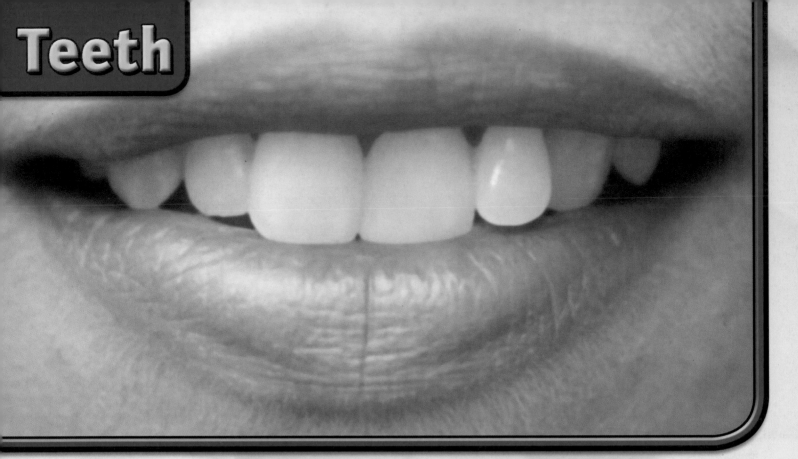

Look in the mirror and smile. Do you have beautiful white teeth? Open wide and count your teeth. If you haven't lost any of your baby teeth, you probably have 20 teeth (although some children can have extra baby teeth). If you count your parents' teeth, they usually have 28 (or 32 if their wisdom teeth haven't been removed).

Enamel (310X)

The protective coating on a tooth is the enamel; it is the white you see on teeth. The image above is an enlarged area of tooth enamel with plaque coated on it. The plaque will eventually erode the tooth. When properly cared for, the enamel of a tooth will last a person's entire life.

Take a close look at the illustration of the tooth on the right. The top part of your tooth, sticking out from your gums, is called the *crown,* and the white, shiny, hard stuff on the surface is called the *enamel.* If you could remove the enamel, you would find another layer called the *dentin.* This layer is dense and bonelike.

Digging even deeper into your tooth, you would find the *pulp,* which pretty much lives up to its name—it is pulpy, like mashed potatoes. The pulp holds the nerve endings, which are what cause you pain when you have a toothache. If you've never had a toothache, have you ever eaten something really cold that hurt your teeth? The nerves in your pulp tell your brain that you are eating something that is too cold.

The pulp and the dentin don't just stop at the gum line like the enamel does—they continue down below the gums into the *root* of your tooth. Teeth are a bit like trees—the larger teeth have deeper roots.

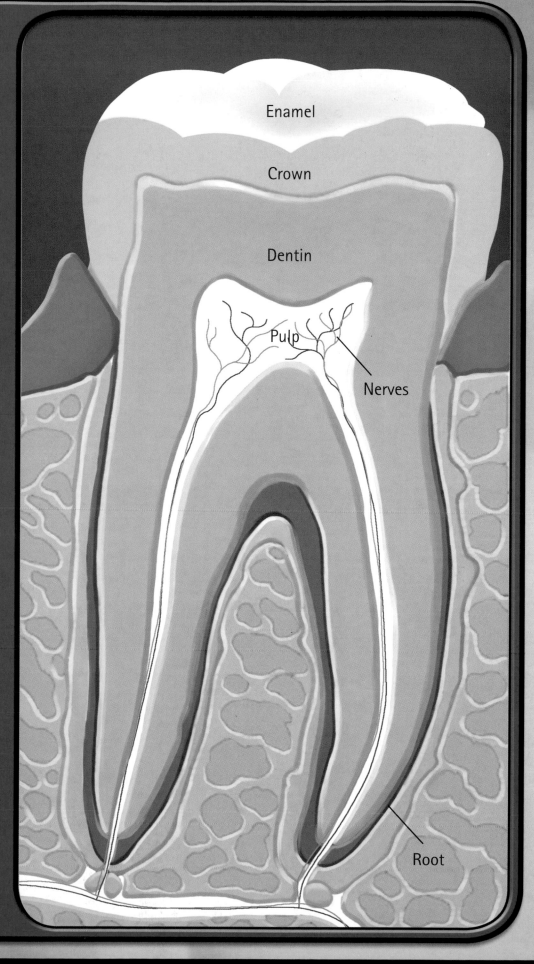

Enamel

Crown

Dentin

Pulp

Nerves

Root

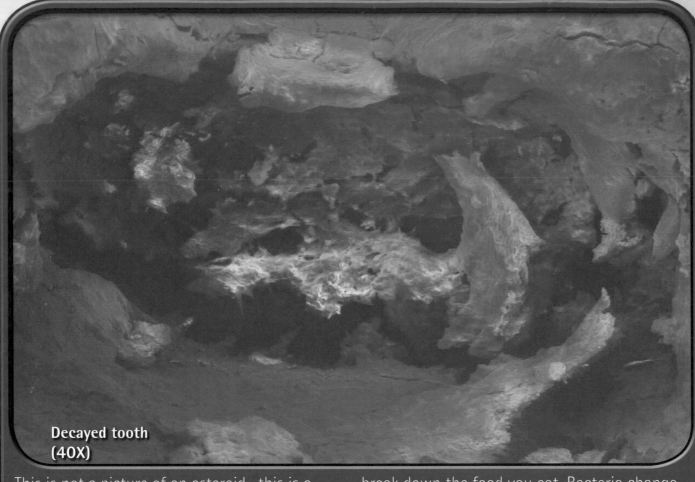

**Decayed tooth
(40X)**

This is not a picture of an asteroid—this is a decayed tooth. The deep pits are cavities caused by plaque. How can this happen?

Scientists have identified at least 80 types of bacteria that live in your mouth. These germs break down the food you eat. Bacteria change sugars—from candy or sweets—into acids. Great, now what? If the bacteria aren't removed from your mouth by—you guessed it—brushing and flossing, they can cause tooth decay.

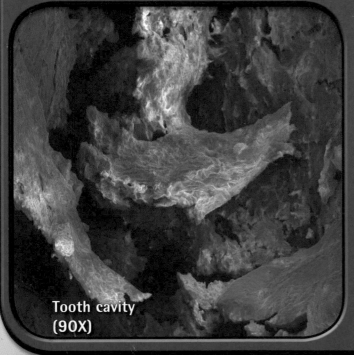

**Tooth cavity
(90X)**

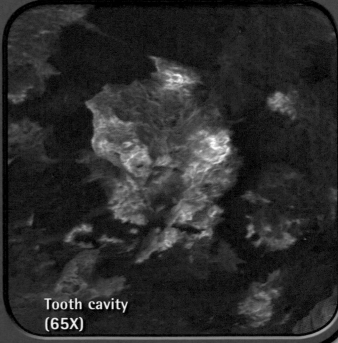

**Tooth cavity
(65X)**

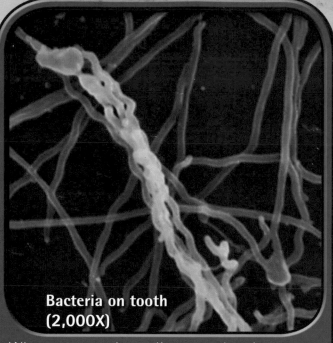

Bacteria on tooth (2,000X)

When your mother tells you to brush your teeth because you are growing things on them, you probably think she is just kidding. Run your tongue over your teeth now. Do they feel smooth or slimy? The slimy feeling is not a good sign. It turns out your mother is right—you ARE growing things on your teeth, and this is what they look like!

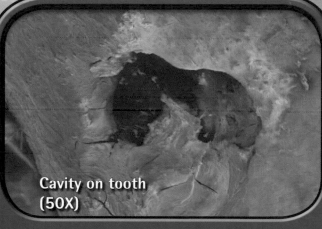

Cavity on tooth (50X)

Without proper brushing, flossing, and general care, plaque soon gets the better of your teeth. It begins to eat away at the enamel, and then continues to gnaw its way through your teeth. If a dentist doesn't treat this, the tooth will soon be destroyed and the dentist will have to extract it.

Note to parents:
If these pictures don't encourage your child to change his or her oral hygiene habits, nothing ever will. You might want to hang this page next to the bathroom mirror above the toothbrush!

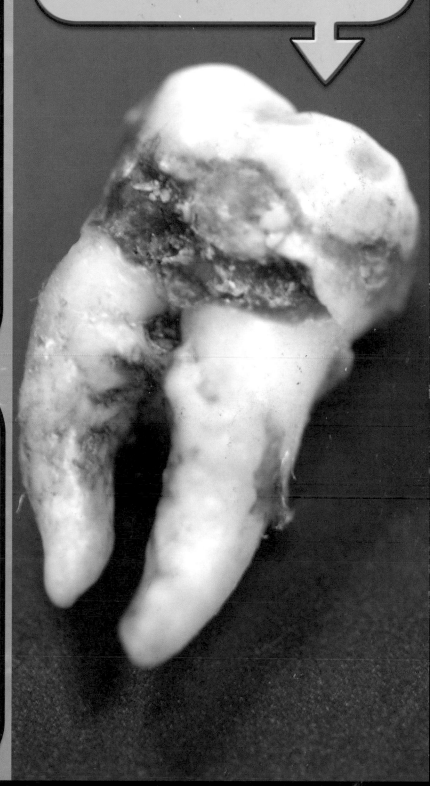

Taste

Do you have good gustation? "Gustation" is a scientific word that simply means the sense of taste or the act of tasting. There are four basic tastes: salty, sweet, sour, and bitter.

This may be the only time when it is polite to stick out your tongue. If you've been eating colorful candy, you might want to brush your teeth and rinse your mouth before studying your tongue. Use a magnifying mirror if you have one—the kind used for putting on makeup or for shaving—and take a close look at your tongue. Can you find tiny bumps on its surface?

COUNTING BUDS

Take a swig of milk, then check out your tongue. Are the bumps on it easy to see? These are your taste buds. These bumps are called *papillae*. If you try counting these bumps, it will take you quite a while—there are thousands of them. While the bumps from taste buds are easy to see without a microscope, what do you think they look like up close?

Human tongue and taste buds

These are taste buds. No, we can't tell you which type of taste buds they are, because they don't work that way. There was a time when it was popular to make a "tongue map." You would place different samples of liquid on your tongue—something salty, for example—and see if your tongue was more receptive to this taste in one particular spot. This is only a myth, as your tongue is equally sensitive to every taste over its entire surface.

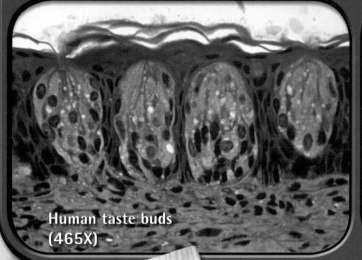

Human taste buds
(465X)

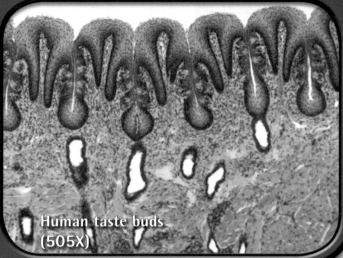

Human taste buds
(505X)

THE FIFTH TASTE

Scientists have identified a fifth taste that the brain can recognize: *umami*. What does umami taste like? According to recent research, umami tastes like glutamate, the flavor in MSG (monosodium glutamate). While many people can taste umami, only the Japanese have a word to describe it. The translation of the word means "meaty" or "savory."

Did you know?

Taste and smell go hand in hand. If you've ever had a cold or a stuffy nose, you probably couldn't taste much. In fact, if you closed your eyes and held your nose closed, you might not be able to tell if you were eating an apple or an onion.

Lungs

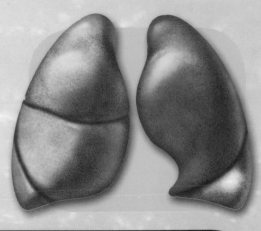

The picture below looks like a magnified piece of a kitchen sponge. Guess again. What you are looking at is part of a human lung. This section is called the *alveoli* (al-VEE-o-lie). Alveoli are air sacs used for the exchange of oxygen and carbon dioxide. There are about 700 million of them in your lungs. These delicate sacs can be easily damaged, especially by cigarette smoke.

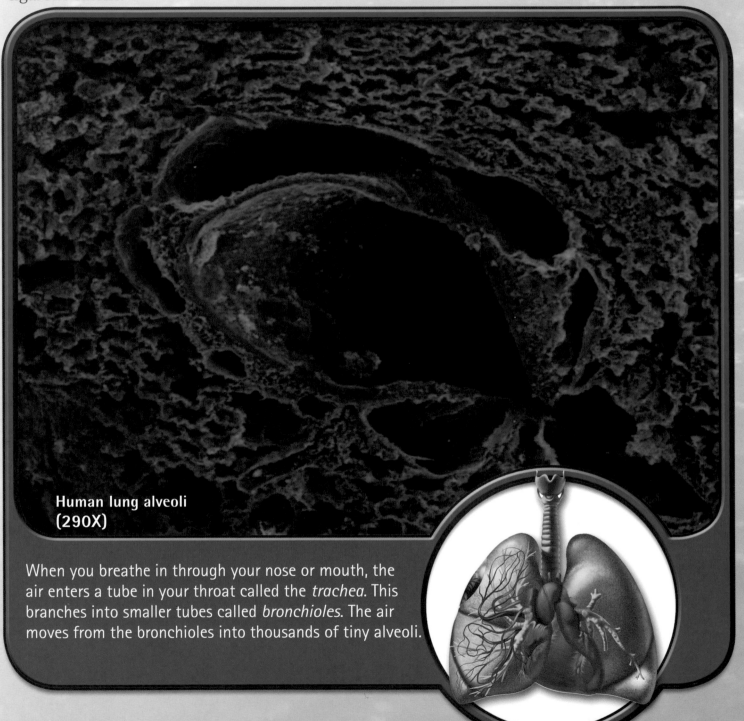

**Human lung alveoli
(290X)**

When you breathe in through your nose or mouth, the air enters a tube in your throat called the *trachea*. This branches into smaller tubes called *bronchioles*. The air moves from the bronchioles into thousands of tiny alveoli.

Alveoli have a spongelike shape for a good reason. This shape allows the lung cells to cover the largest amount of space possible. The greater the area of the lung in contact with the air you breathe, the faster the lungs can take in the oxygen you need and get rid of the carbon dioxide that your body makes. The air you breathe is about 21 percent oxygen. You use up a small portion of oxygen with each breath you take. The oxygen goes into your lungs, then passes through the thin lining of the lungs and into your bloodstream. In your bloodstream it attaches itself to your red blood cells (see page 44) and travels throughout your body. Your body uses the oxygen in your blood with sugars from the foods you eat to give you energy. The carbon dioxide that you exhale is a waste product.

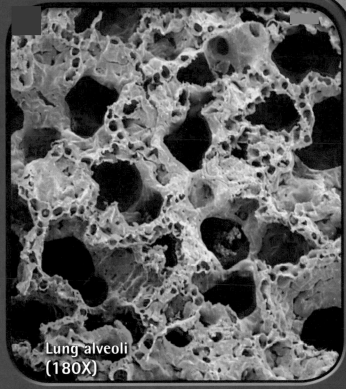
Lung alveoli
(180X)

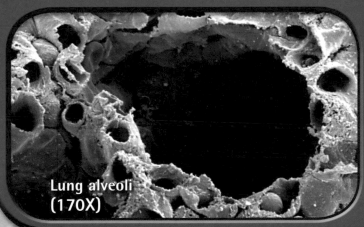
Lung alveoli
(170X)

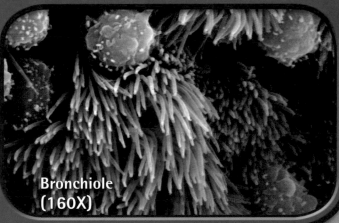
Bronchiole
(160X)

Did you know?

When we breathe in, we fill up our lungs like a balloon, but when we breathe out, why don't our lungs collapse like an empty balloon? The secret to this is in the types of cells that make up the inside of the tiny alveoli in our lungs. There are two types of cells, cleverly called type 1 and type 2. Type 1 cells allow oxygen to enter and carbon dioxide to leave the lungs. These cells are thin and smooth. Type 2 cells give off a type of lipid molecules called *surfactant molecules*. These molecules combine with water to make the alveoli less sticky, so they don't collapse together when they are emptied of air.

Bronchioles into the lung's alveoli

Intestines

LINING OF THE INTESTINE

This is what it looks like inside your small intestine. The tiny cone-shaped projections are called *villi*. The villi are covered with smaller projections called *microvilli*. Each villus contains a column of cells that absorb the nutrients from the food you eat.

Intestinal villi
(575X)

WHERE ARE YOUR INTESTINES?

If you put your hands on your hips with your fingers pointed toward your middle, you are pointing at them. Your intestines are part of your digestive system. When food goes into your mouth, it travels through your throat to your stomach through a tube called the *esophagus*. In your stomach, the food gets churned up with acids and enzymes and is broken down into a slushy mixture. This mixture then goes into your small intestine, which finishes digesting the food and absorbs from it the important nutrients your body needs. Once your body has finished with the food, the remainder—the waste material—travels down through the large intestine and out the body via the anus in the form of feces, or poop. The longest of the body's internal organs, the small intestine measures an average of 20 feet long; the large intestine's length averages about five feet.

Intestinal villi
(465X)

YET ANOTHER REASON TO EAT YOUR MEAT WELL DONE!

Truth is stranger than fiction—and in this case, yuckier. If you eat improperly cooked meat, you could become host to the lovely and charming beef tapeworm *Taenia saginata*. This creature will attach itself to the walls of your small intestine, where it begins to grow and grow and grow. How long can this thing get? The tapeworm can grow the length of your small and large intestine!

E. coli Bacteria

If you're not a vegetarian, this looks like a pretty good meal. But did you know that lurking in this seemingly harmless hamburger could be bacteria that can kill you?

E. coli bacteria
(140X)

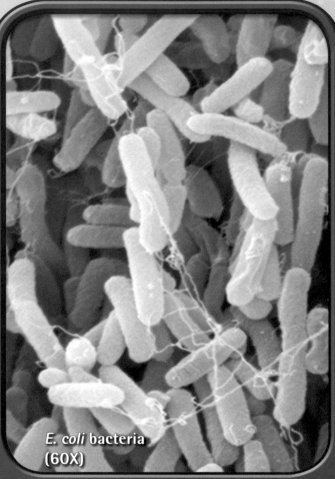

E. coli bacteria
(60X)

Some things need to be cooked really well or you can get sick from eating them. The *E. coli* bacteria are sometimes found in undercooked hamburger meat or meat that has not been stored at the correct temperature (33 degrees Fahrenheit). This is not to say that eating an undercooked hamburger will always make you ill, but you have a better chance of getting sick if the meat is not cooked to a temperature that would kill these bacteria (160 degrees Fahrenheit).

What is *E. coli* and where does it come from? *E. coli* is the shortened name for the microorganism *Escherichia coli*. You can get the virus from a number of different sources, but the most common are eating ground beef that is undercooked or drinking water that is unclean. Once infected with *E. coli*, you can easily pass it on to other people—even if they aren't eating or drinking the same things as you.

How can you tell if you have an *E. coli* infection? Well, you'd be really sick with fever, queasiness, vomiting, cramps, and sometimes bloody diarrhea. You would need to get to a doctor as soon as possible. Have we scared you enough? Will you now promise to wash your hands and eat your hamburger well done?

If you don't want to become ill due to these germs, here are a few easy things you can do:

- Avoid eating raw or undercooked hamburger meat. No pink!

- Wash your hands.

- Ask your parents not to place raw meat next to cooked meat, and ask them to defrost meat in the fridge, not on the counter.

- Eat hot foods when they are hot and cold foods when they are cold. Fruit, bread, and cookies are good at room temperature, but other things may not be. Check with an adult if you aren't sure if something has gone bad. When in doubt, don't eat it.

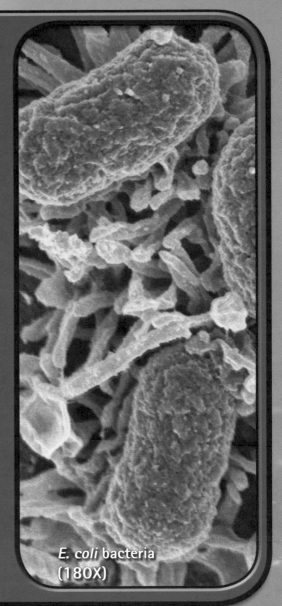

E. coli bacteria
(180X)

Did you know?

Wash your hands! There are several different strains of *E. coli* and some are much more harmful than others. *E. coli* is a normal inhabitant of your digestive system and lives there quite happily. When it moves to a part of your body it doesn't normally occupy, it can cause problems. This can happen if you don't cleanse your hands after you go to the bathroom—the *E. coli* can be transferred to your mouth or other body parts. So, keep your hands clean and *E. coli* will not cause you grief!

Red Blood Cells

Red blood cells are something you cannot live without! Zipping around your body, they snap up the oxygen from the air you breathe into your lungs and distribute it to all parts of your body. They are shaped like breath mints, thicker around the edge and thinner in the middle; this is called a *biconcave* shape. The biconcave shape allows the red blood cells to squeeze through tiny capillaries and travel right out to the tips of your fingers and toes.

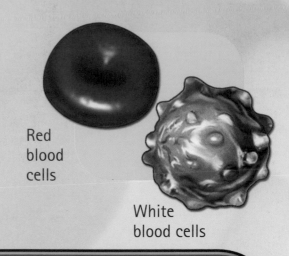

Red blood cells

White blood cells

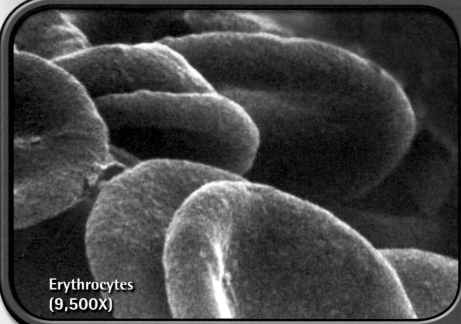

Erythrocytes (9,500X)

Red blood cells—also called *erythrocytes*—are very tiny, about 0.0075 millimeter in diameter. In fact, one cubic millimeter of blood contains about five million red blood cells. They are different from most types of cells in your body because they don't contain a *nucleus*. This is a small structure found in most cells that coordinates the cell's activities.

Red blood cells are made in the bone marrow found inside your bones. They live for about 120 days. When they get too old, your spleen—located behind your stomach on the left side of your body—breaks down the old cells. The remains are then transported elsewhere in your body, where they are either excreted or recycled to manufacture new blood cells.

Bone marrow (200X)

The reason that red blood cells are red is because they contain a chemical called *hemoglobin*. This chemical is red when your blood contains lots of oxygen and it becomes a purple-blue color when the oxygen has been exchanged for carbon dioxide. If you look at the inside of your wrist, you may see some purple and blue lines. These are the blood vessels under your skin. The difference in the colors of these blood vessels is caused partly by the amount of oxygen in the blood traveling through them.

Red blood cells (8,500X)

Did you know?

When you were still inside your mother's womb, your red blood cells had a unique kind of hemoglobin. This fetal hemoglobin is designed to take in oxygen from the mother's blood. It is only found in the blood of fetuses and newborn babies. After you were born, the hemoglobin in your blood cells began to be replaced with regular hemoglobin.

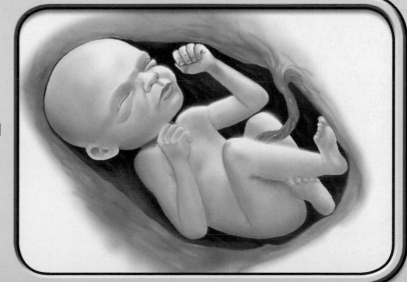

Bones

You probably don't think too much about your bones . . . until you take a good tumble and break one. Then your bones matter a great deal. So what are bones and how do you care for them?

If you were to look just at one of your bones—let's say the humerus, or upper arm bone—you would see a thin, flexible outer coating called the *periosteum*. This is made from connective tissue. Inside this layer are two types of bone: *spongy bone* and *compact bone*.

Spongy bone (850X)

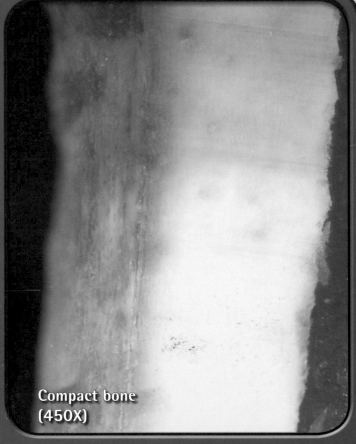

Compact bone (450X)

Spongy bone, much like its name, looks like a sponge, with lots of pockets or spaces filled with soft tissue. The cells that make the hard part of the bone are called *osteocytes* and are arranged along lines of stress. This is why you can't stay in bed after you have broken your leg. Doctors want you to get up and move, to put some stress back on your bones to help them heal faster.

Compact bone is thick with densely packed bone cells. Although it looks like it isn't alive, this type of bone contains osteocytes that are actively working. Most of this bone is made from a matrix, or framework, of collagen, a type of protein that forms fibers with a mineral called *calcium phosphate*.

WHAT HAPPENS IF YOU DON'T TAKE CARE OF YOUR BONES?

A condition called *osteoporosis* can cause your bones to become brittle and break easily. Usually seen only in older people, this condition is becoming more common in younger people. Once this happens, it is very hard to heal your bones, so make sure you start taking care of your bones now, while you are young.

Healthy leg bone (520X)

HOW TO HAVE HEALTHY BONES

Your bones contain calcium phosphate. When your body needs calcium, it can take it from your bones. As long as you are eating and drinking enough foods that contain calcium, the calcium your body needs will come from your food and not from your bones. To have healthy bones, you need to do two things: make sure you get sufficient calcium from your diet, and make sure your bones get enough exercise. What kinds of foods contain calcium? Milk is a good source, as are milk products such as cheese and yogurt. Soda pop not only doesn't contain calcium, it can actually remove calcium from your body, so it isn't a good thing to include in your regular diet. Save the soda for special occasions. How can you exercise your bones? Almost any kind of exercise is good, even walking. You don't need to work out all the time, but anything that stresses your bones will do.

Brittle bone (500X)

Glossary

Alveoli: The primary gas exchange units of the lung.

Aqueous humor: The fluid that maintains the shape of the front part of the eye.

Biconcave: Concave, or curved like the inner surface of a sphere, on both sides.

Bronchioles: The smallest tubes of the lungs.

Calcium: A component found in food, such as dairy products, that help to strengthen bones and teeth.

Cavity: Pits in a tooth caused by plaque; primarily from sugary foods and drinks.

Collagen: The sinewy substance that joins the bones and muscles together.

Compact bone: Outer bone that makes up a large portion of skeletal mass.

Cortex: The main layer inside a strand of hair.

Crown: The portion of the tooth that rises above the gums.

Demodicids: A type of mite that lives and breeds on eyelashes.

Dermatitis: Inflammation of the skin.

Enamel: The hard surface of the tooth.

Epidermis: The outermost layer of the skin.

Erythrocytes: Red blood cells.

Esophagus: The tube that allows the passage of food down to the stomach.

Fibrin: A sticky, fibrous protein that assists in blood coagulation.

Fibrinogen: A blood plasma protein essential for the coagulation, or thickening, of blood.

Follicle: A tiny body cavity that holds the hair root.

Gustation: The act of tasting.

Hemoglobin: The respiratory pigment in blood cells that causes the red color.

Lunula: The white, moon-shaped area at the bottom of a toenail or fingernail.

Matrix: The formative cells of a fingernail, toenail, tooth, or hair.

Medulla: The inner core of certain body structures such as bones and hair.

Melanocyte: The cells that produce melanin, the pigment responsible for hair color.

Microvilli: Tiny hairlike structures that protrude from the small intestine.

Osteocytes: The branched cells that make up the hard portion of the bone.

Osteoporosis: A condition that can cause bones to become brittle and break easily.

Papillae: The bumpy taste buds that blanket the surface of the tongue.

Periosteum: The fibrous covering of a bone.

Platelets: Tiny blood particles that promote blood clotting.

Pulp: The mushy center of a tooth.

Resilin: An elastic substance found in the skin of many insects.

Root: The portion of the tooth below the gums.

Seborrheic dermatitis: A disease that results in scaling on the skin, like dandruff.

Serum: The watery portion of the blood.

Shaft: The section of a hair that projects from the surface of the body.

Spongy bone: The porous, soft part of the inner bone.

Tapeworm: A parasite that gestates within the intestines of animals and humans.

Thrombin: An enzyme in blood that converts fibrinogen to fibrin during blood clotting.

Trachea: The tube that carries air to the lungs; also called the *windpipe*.

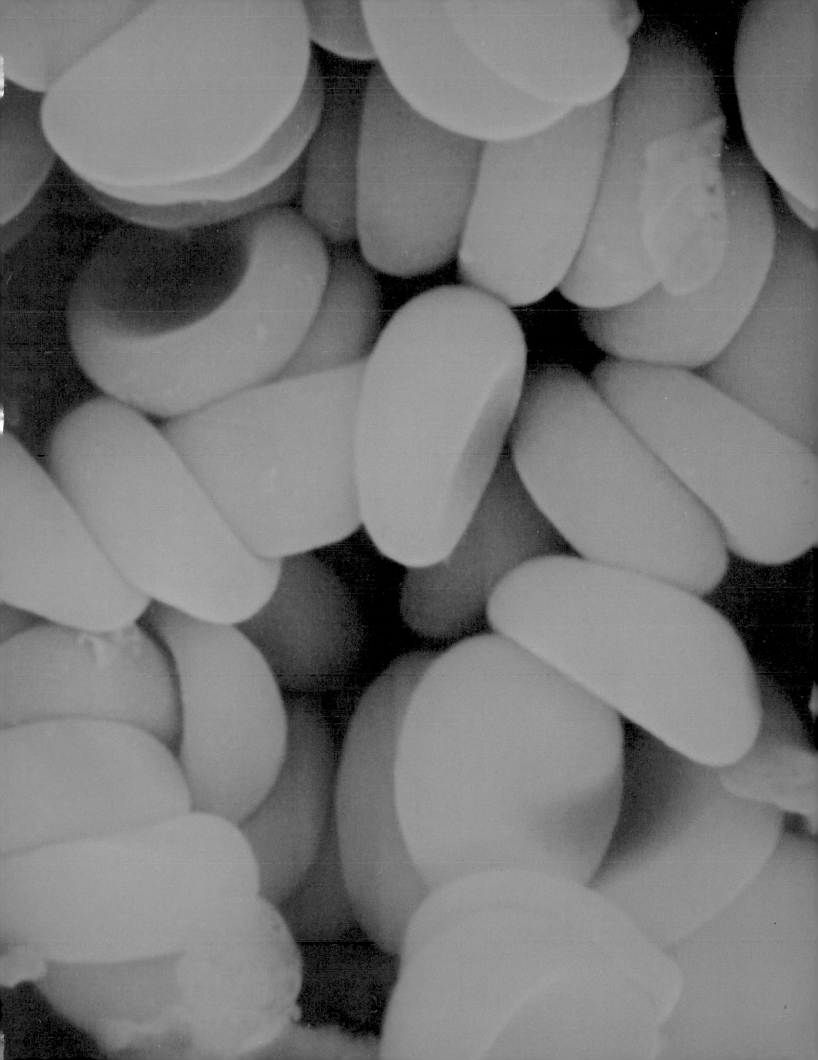

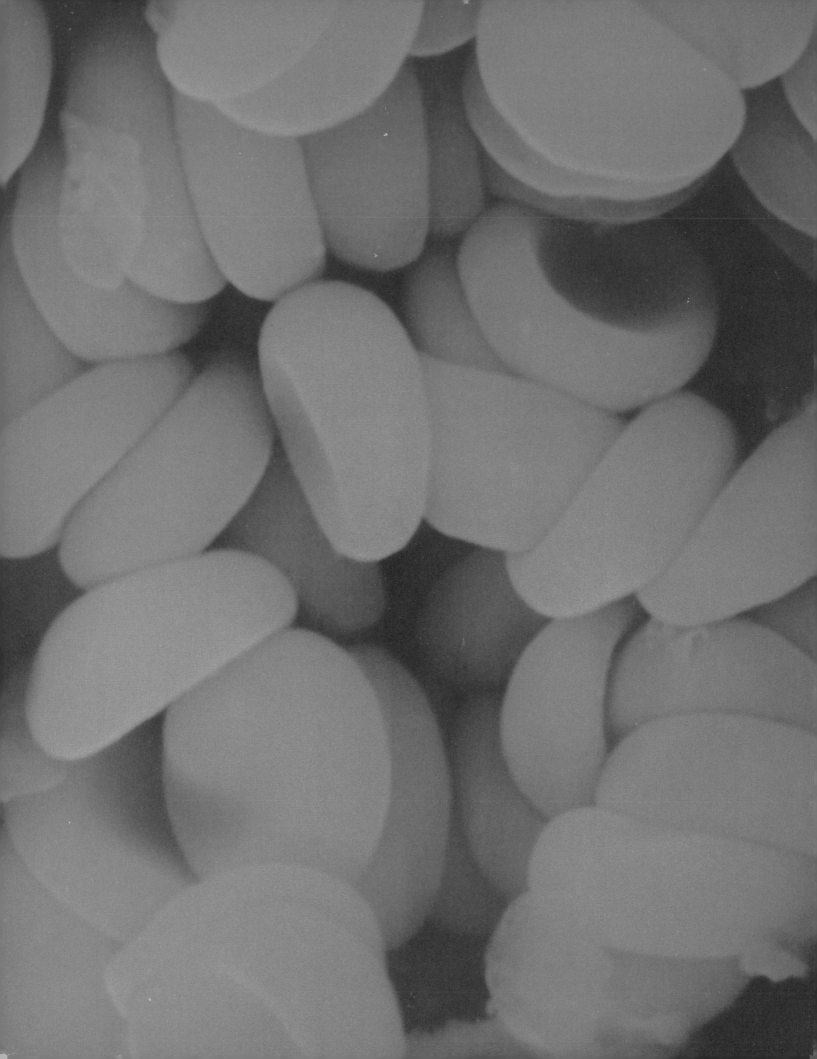